Where Is It?

Characters

Mona - An 8-year-old girl
Sam - Mona's younger brother
Mum

Where Is It?

Mona's lounge. Sam is sitting on the sofa reading a comic. Enter Mona. She snatches Sam's comic.

Sam   Oi! I was reading that.

Mona   *(angrily)* Where is it?

Sam   Where's what?

Mona   You know what.

Sam   What?

Mona   You know what it is and you know where
you've put it.

Sam   But I don't know what it is, so I don't know
where I've put it.

Mona   Don't lie! Where have you put it?

Sam   *(totally confused)* Where have I put what?

5

Mona I don't know where you've put it. But you've put it somewhere.

Sam I don't know what you're talking about!

Mona What?

Sam Don't you start with the 'what' thing. Just tell me what you are going on about.

Mona *(taking a deep breath)* You've had my
Gamestation and put it somewhere. That's what.

Sam I haven't touched your Gamestation.

Mona Don't lie. You must have it.

Sam Why would I want your Gamestation? It's got
rubbish games on it.

Mona What! You wouldn't know a good game if it hit
you in the head.

Sam It wouldn't be good if it hit me in the head. It
would be bad!

Mona   Stop changing the subject. Where have you put my Gamestation?

Sam   I haven't got it. You must have left it somewhere. Where did you have it last?

Mona   If I knew that, it wouldn't be lost because
            I'd know where it was!

Sam   So you must have lost it then.

Mona   I don't lose things. You've got it. I'm
            telling Mum. *(shouting)* MUM!!

Enter Mum. She is holding a Gamestation.

Mum   Oh, Mona ... I was cleaning under your bed. Did you know your Gamestation was there?

Mona   *(quickly)* Of course I did.

Sam   *(shocked)* What?!

Mum   Now, what did you want?

Mona   *(smiling)* Oh, nothing ...

Do I Have To?

Characters

Mona – an 8-year-old girl
Mum

Do I Have To?

Mona's kitchen. Mum is packing a bag with biscuits and cakes. Enter Mona.

Mum   Are you ready yet? Gran will be here soon.

Mona   Oh, Mum! Do I have to go?

Mum   Don't start moaning, Mona. We've been through this. You're going.

Mona   Why?

Mum   Because Gran wants to take you to Auntie Doreen's party at the old people's home.

Mona   But do I have to?

Mum   Yes, you do!

Mona   But why do I have to?

Mum   Because you do.

Mona   That's not a proper answer.

Mum   It's proper enough for you.

Mona   Old people always say things like that. When I'm old, I won't say that to my kids!

Mum   I bet you will.

Mona   But why do I have to go?

Mum   Because Gran asked you to go and it's a nice thing to do.

Mona If it's nice, why aren't you going?

Mum Er, I'm busy …

Mona So am I!

Mum Eating cookies is not what I'd call 'busy'!

Mona   Well, why can't Sam go?

Mum   He's out with Dad. You're going and that's that.

Mona   Adults always say that as well.

Mum   Then you should be used to it.

Mona   The last time I went to one of those parties, it was BORING! All we did was sit around with all the old people.

Mum   You'll be old in the future.

Mona   No I won't.

Mum   But didn't you just say, *(putting on Mona's voice)*, 'When I'm old, I won't say that to my kids!'?

Mona   Well, I won't!

There is a knock on the door.

Mum Gran is here. Take this bag. And have a nice time.

Mona *(sulking)* I won't.

Mona exits. The lights go out.

After a few minutes, the lights go up. It is now evening and we are in Mona's kitchen. Mum is reading a magazine. Enter Mona.

Mum   So, how was the party?

Mona   *(quickly)* It was brilliant! We played bingo. Then we had a sing-song and I won a prize for being the best singer. And the food was scrummy! And Auntie Doreen told a rude joke! I can't wait until I get older!

Mum So all your moaning was over nothing!

Mona Moaning? What moaning? I never moan!

Are We Nearly There Yet?

Characters

Mona – an 8-year-old girl
Sam – Mona's younger brother
Mum

Are We Nearly There Yet?

Mum is driving the car. The car is stuck in traffic. Sam and Mona are in the back of the car.

Mona   Are we nearly there yet?

Mum   No.

Mona   We've been sitting here for hours!

Mum   I'm sorry but there's a lot of traffic.

Mona makes a face at Sam. Sam makes a face back at Mona. Mona pinches Sam.

Sam   Mum, Mona pinched me!

Mona   He made a face at me. Like this! *(She makes a face.)*

Sam   She started it.

Mona   Did not.

Sam   Did too.

Mona   Did not …

Mum Stop it, you two! I'll tell you what, let's play 'I Spy'. Sam can start.

Sam I spy with my little eye, something beginning with 'C'.

Mona *(in a bored voice)* Car.

Sam *(disappointed)* Oh! You guessed it.

Mona My turn. I spy with my little eye, something beginning with 'DGTJTGOFM'.

Sam You can't have all those letters!

Mona Give up? It's 'Dirty Great Traffic Jam That Goes On For Miles'.

Sam You cheated!

Mona Did not.

Sam Did too.

Mona Did not ...

Mum (*annoyed*) I'm going to scream in a minute! Mona, why don't you listen to some music?

Mona I've heard every tune already.

Mum Well, play a game on your Gamestation.

Mona I've got to the top level on all of them.

Mum Read a book then.

Mona I've read them all. Twice.

Mum (*shouting*) Well then, just sit still and be quiet! (*Mona sulks*) At last! The traffic jam is moving.

The car starts to move.

Mona   I never wanted to go to the seaside anyway.
There's never any sun, you get sand in your
knickers, seagulls poo on you …

Mum   Didn't I say be quiet? I'm sure I said be quiet.

Sam   Yes, you did. Be quiet, Mona.

Mona   Oh, OK. I'll be quiet …

There is a pause.

Mona   Are we nearly there yet?

Mum   No.

There is another pause.

Mona   Are we nearly there yet?

Mum   No.

There is an even longer pause.

Mona Are we nearly there yet?

A smile breaks out over Mum's face. She stops the car.

Mum Yes. We're here.

Mona gets out of the car.

Mona   This is going to be SO boring. This is going to be
… oh, hang on! The sun's out … look how blue
the sea is … can I have an ice cream? Where's
my bucket and spade? Come on, Sam! Last one
on the beach is a jellyfish! I'm so glad we came!

*Mona and Sam run off. Mum collapses over the steering
wheel with a groan.*